To Nadia and Adam,
who hold the future in their hands and hearts
—KLA

To Eva Jane and Leo Paul with love
—SLR

Hands Around the Library
Protecting Egypt's Treasured Books

by **Susan L. Roth** and
Karen Leggett Abouraya

collages by **Susan L. Roth**

Dial Books for Young Readers ✦ an imprint of Penguin Group (USA) Inc.

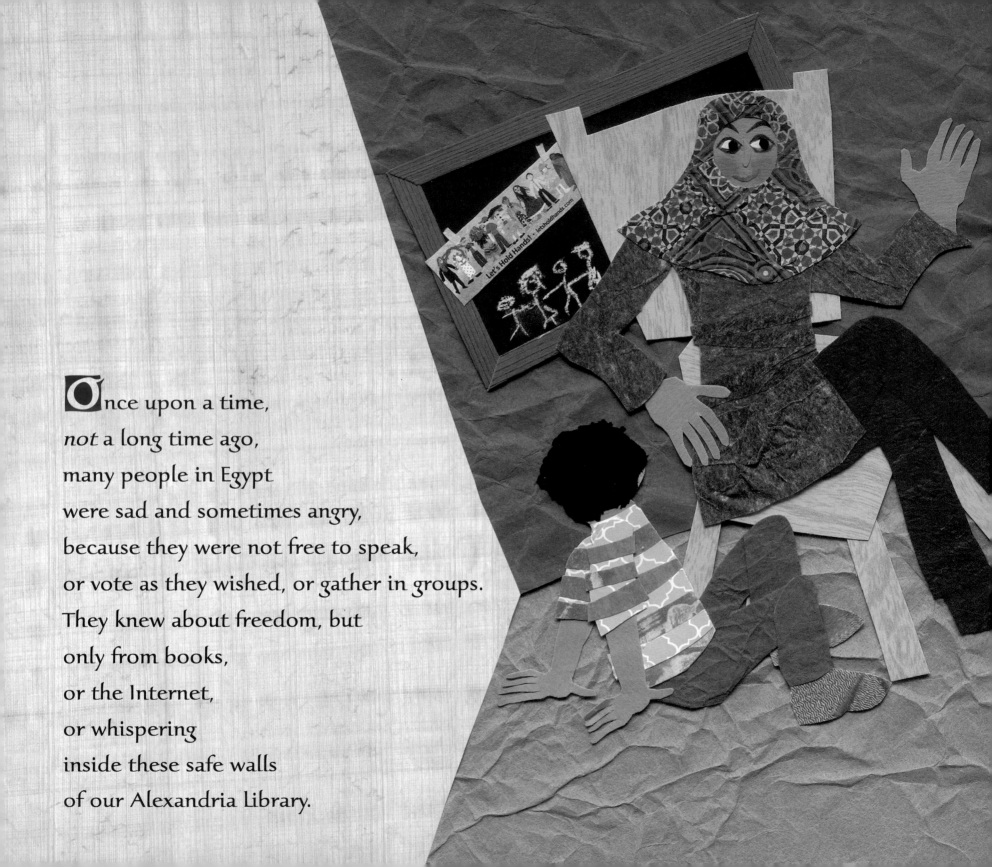

Once upon a time,
not a long time ago,
many people in Egypt
were sad and sometimes angry,
because they were not free to speak,
or vote as they wished, or gather in groups.
They knew about freedom, but
only from books,
or the Internet,
or whispering
inside these safe walls
of our Alexandria Library.

Egypt's young people decided
it was finally time
to let their voices be heard,
and so they began to march in the streets.

First they marched in Cairo,
but soon they marched in Alexandria too.
They raised their voices,
and many others followed.

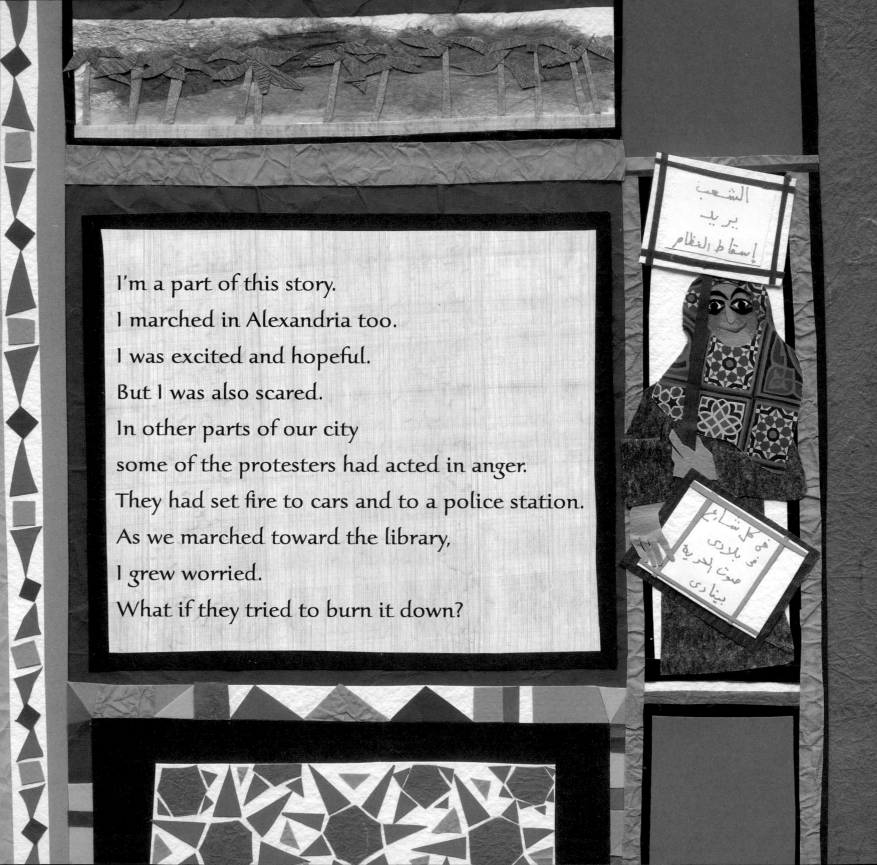

I'm a part of this story.

I marched in Alexandria too.

I was excited and hopeful.

But I was also scared.

In other parts of our city

some of the protesters had acted in anger.

They had set fire to cars and to a police station.

As we marched toward the library,

I grew worried.

What if they tried to burn it down?

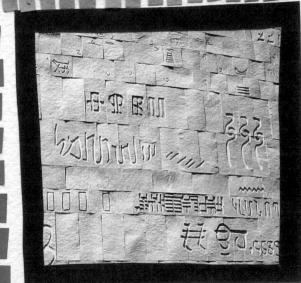

Our Alexandria Library,
built on the ashes of the ancient, famous one,
is the most beautiful modern building in
all of Egypt.
Our ancient Egyptian stories
are kept alive here,
in the books,
and in the carved stone
and shimmering glass
of the building itself.
We were free inside the library
even when we were not free outside.
We could not let our Alexandria Library burn!

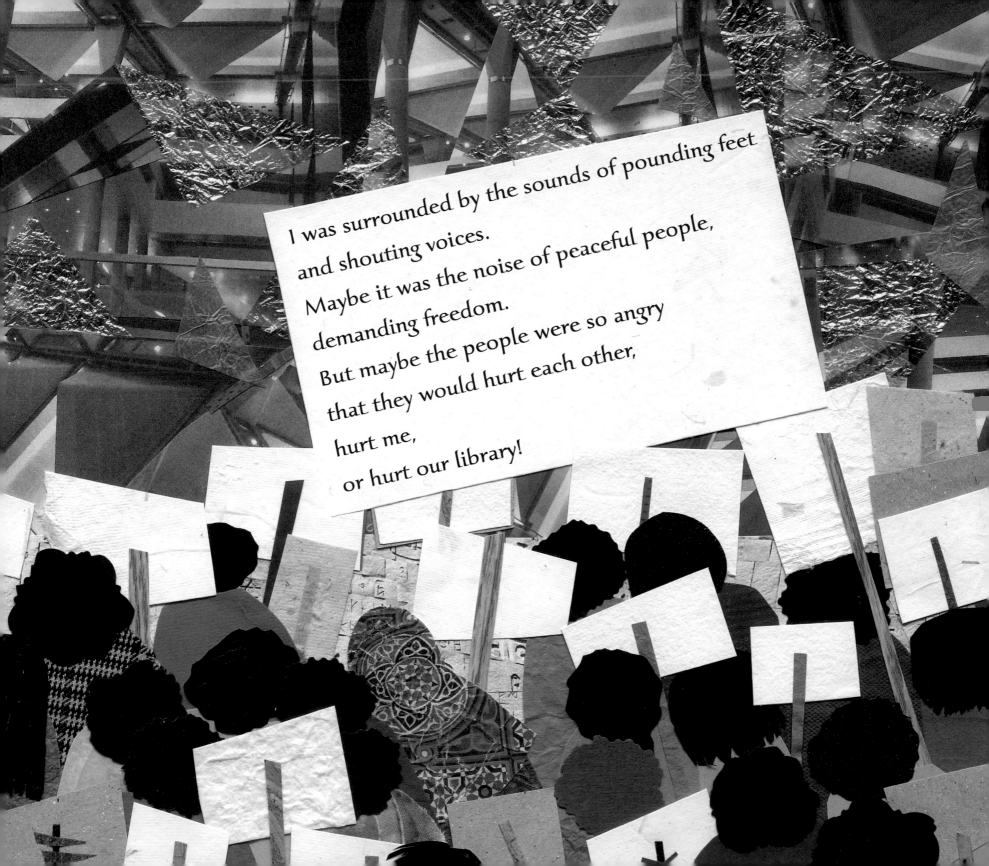

I was surrounded by the sounds of pounding feet
and shouting voices.
Maybe it was the noise of peaceful people,
demanding freedom.
But maybe the people were so angry
that they would hurt each other,
hurt me,
or hurt our library!

Thousands of us were
marching for freedom,
as if caught on a wave
from the Mediterranean Sea.
Dr. Ismail Serageldin, the library director,
saw us approaching.
"The library has no gates that can be locked,"
he called out.
"The doors are all glass.
There is nothing that prevents anybody
from destroying this building
with all its treasures,
except the will of the people."

The marchers pushed together
closer and closer to the library.
The crowd surged around me on the sidewalk,
shouting and waving signs.
We were in front of the library.
We were on the library steps.
The shouting grew louder.
Then a young man broke from the marchers.
He ran up the steps to Dr. Serageldin . . .

. . . and he took hold
of the director's hand!
A young girl followed.
She took Dr. Serageldin's other hand.
And then there were five,
then six, then seven, then ten,
all holding hands,
protecting the library.

Then I too broke into the chain
that was stretching
farther and farther,
turning around the library,
reaching toward the sea.

When some of the marchers spread
a huge Egyptian flag across the steps,
people cried together:
"WE LOVE YOU, EGYPT!"

A little boy held up another Egyptian flag.
It was twice as tall as he was. He waved it
right in front of Dr. Ismail Serageldin.
A smile crinkled the director's face as he spoke.
"Thank you for protecting our library with us.
Go forth into the journey of your lives
and create a better world!
"Thank you," he said, his voice catching a little.
"Thank you from the bottom of my heart."

That day the whole world heard
his words
and watched
our Alexandria Library,
our Bibliotheca Alexandrina,
with all our people
holding hands
in the perfect circle
surrounding it.

And because together
we all protected
our Bibliotheca Alexandrina,
once upon a time
not a long time ago,
the library still stands today
holding all of our stories.

Bibliotheca Alexandrina

Bibliotheca Alexandrina

Left: Young Egyptians break away from the march to hold hands around the library and its planetarium.

Right: Egyptians of all ages and religions hold a giant national flag on the steps of the library.

library director Ismail Serageldin (gray jacket in the middle) waves to Egyptian marchers outside the library, while young children wave their own flags of support.

Bibliotheca Alexandrina

Bibliotheca Alexandrina

Susan L. Roth

Left: Former librarian Shaimaa Saad in the Children's library

Right: Young People's Library in Bibliotheca Alexandrina

Bibliotheca Alexandrina

Bibliotheca Alexandrina

Left: The slanted roof of the library allows sunlight to fill the space inside.

Right: The granite wall outside the library displays hand-carved characters and letters from all cultures, alphabets, and eras.

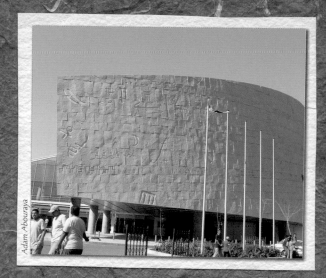

Adam Abouraya

An architect from Norway designed the library to give visitors a feeling of openness and discovery on each floor.

Adam Abouraya

Adam Abouraya

Adam Abouraya

Bibliotheca Alexandrina

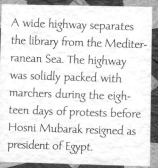

A wide highway separates the library from the Mediterranean Sea. The highway was solidly packed with marchers during the eighteen days of protests before Hosni Mubarak resigned as president of Egypt.

Alexandria, Then and Now

Ancient Library

The library protected by the Egyptian marchers is close to the place where there was an awesome ancient library.

A king named Ptolemy wanted to collect all the knowledge of the world in one place, so he built the Great library of Alexandria about 2,300 years ago. Ships coming to the port of Alexandria were ordered to give their scrolls to the library, where they were then copied by scribes. The scrolls were made of papyrus, a grass that grew easily along the Nile River in Egypt.

From 300 BCE until 400 CE, the library was a center where great thinkers, scientists, mathematicians, and poets came to study and share ideas. There was even a zoo where scientists could study animals like crocodiles.

No one knows for sure what happened to the ancient library. One story says the Roman emperor Julius Caesar set fire to Egyptian ships in the harbor of Alexandria, and wind carried the fire to the library. Other stories blame either Christian or Muslim leaders for burning books that did not agree with what they believed.

Modern Library

The new Bibliotheca Alexandrina—with the same Latin name as the ancient library—opened in 2002.

The sun was an important symbol in ancient Egypt, and the circle shape of the new building represents the sun shining on the world. All around the outside of the building are four thousand blocks of granite from Aswan, a town on the Nile River in the south of Egypt. Each stone is carved with a letter or a sign from five hundred different alphabets.

This new library has seven floors aboveground and four floors underground. There is a brand-new

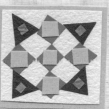

planetarium—just like there was in the ancient library—but no zoo!

The library already has more than a million books. There is a children's library with a special section for children with disabilities. There are classes in Arabic handwriting, mapmaking, and playing ancient Egyptian musical instruments.

Librarian Shaimaa Saad says young people can "read, chat, make friends, dream about the future, think creatively, talk, and discuss all about personal, political, and whatever issues are racing through their minds."

In 2010, fourth graders in Alexandria, Egypt, "Skyped" on their computers with children in Alexandria, Virginia, and Silver Spring, Maryland. They discovered that they wore the same jeans and T-shirts, they all ate pizza, liked many of the same singers, and even knew some of the same professional wrestlers.

The January 25, 2011, Revolution

On January 25, 2011, Egyptians began marching in the streets in large numbers, first in Tahrir Square in Cairo—"Tahrir" means "liberation" in Arabic—and then in Alexandria and other cities. Many of the protests were organized by young people using Facebook and Twitter. They wanted Hosni Mubarak to resign as president of Egypt, a position he had held for thirty years.

The protests began peacefully, but in the end, more than eight hundred people died. Hosni Mubarak resigned on February 11.

Library director Ismail Serageldin closed the library during the protests, but he said that young people protected it from vandals by forming a ring around it. He said the library helped to spread the democratic ideas that Egyptians were marching for. "In these eighteen days that shook the world, men and women, young and old, Muslims and Christians, rich and poor came together as never before."

Resources

Bibliotheca Alexandrina http://www.bibalex.org/

Sawa, Maureen. *The library Book: The Story of libraries from Camels to Computers*. Illustrated by Bill Slavin. Canada: Tundra Books, 2006

Trumble, Kelly. *The Library of Alexandria*. Illustrated by Robina MacIntyre Marshall. New York: Clarion Books, 2003.

A Few Words from the Protest Signs:

حريه

ho-RAY-ah   Freedom

مصر

Misr   Egypt

بد واحده

yahd WAH-da   One hand

الشعب

Al Shaab   The citizens

الثورة

Al Thorah   The revolution

ديمقراطيه

demo-crah-TAY-a   Democracy

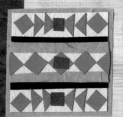

A Note from Susan L. Roth

If my friend Karen Leggett Abouraya hadn't married her Egyptian husband, Tharwat, perhaps she wouldn't know and love Alexandria so much. And certainly if it weren't for Karen's tales of this gorgeous city, I might never have visited Alexandria along with the pyramids and the Sphinx during my first visit to Egypt in 2009.

When my family and I finally arrived at the library, we stood still, dazzled by the extraordinary space. Outside, the sun sparkled on the Mediterranean Sea and Egyptians bought fresh fish to grill for dinner in the same places where they would soon be marching and protecting their library. When Dr. Serageldin wrote with such pride that the library was safe, thanks to Egypt's youth, I knew right then that Karen and I had to tell their story.

While I was at the library in 2009, I met children's librarian Shaimaa Saad, who later conducted several workshops for my *Let's Hold Hands* project (www.letsholdhands.com) with Gary and Kathy Moorman and their group of student teachers from Appalachian State University in North Carolina. The self-portrait collaged paper dolls that the Egyptian children made then have traveled to the Peace Study Center in Baltimore, Maryland, as well as to Appalachian State University. Also, dolls from all over the United States have since been exhibited in the Children's Library at the Bibliotheca Alexandrina.

As always, my international palette of papers and materials knows no boundaries. My materials hold hands under and over barbed wire fences and stone walls and they march right through border controls. Children cannot grow up supporting angry borders if they are taught, from the time they are born, to love books and to hold hands around the world.

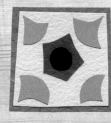

DIAL BOOKS FOR YOUNG READERS
A division of Penguin Young Readers Group
Published by The Penguin Group
Penguin Group (USA) Inc., 375 Hudson Street, New York, NY 10014, U.S.A.
Penguin Group (Canada), 90 Eglinton Avenue East, Suite 700, Toronto, Ontario,
Canada M4P 2Y3 (a division of Pearson Penguin Canada Inc.)
Penguin Books Ltd, 80 Strand, London WC2R 0RL, England
Penguin Ireland, 25 St. Stephen's Green, Dublin 2, Ireland (a division of Penguin Books Ltd)
Penguin Group (Australia), 250 Camberwell Road, Camberwell, Victoria 3124, Australia
(a division of Pearson Australia Group Pty Ltd)
Penguin Books India Pvt Ltd, 11 Community Centre, Panchsheel Park, New Delhi - 110 017, India
Penguin Group (NZ), 67 Apollo Drive, Rosedale, North Shore 0632, New Zealand
(a division of Pearson New Zealand Ltd)
Penguin Books (South Africa) (Pty) Ltd, 24 Sturdee Avenue, Rosebank, Johannesburg 2196, South Africa
Penguin Books Ltd, Registered Offices: 80 Strand, London WC2R 0RL, England

Text copyright © 2012 by Susan L. Roth and Karen Leggett Abouraya
Pictures copyright © 2012 by Susan L. Roth
All rights reserved
The publisher does not have any control over and does not assume any responsibility for author or
third-party websites or their content.
Designed by Jasmin Rubero
Text set in Oxalis Std
Manufactured in China on acid-free paper

10 9

Library of Congress Cataloging-in-Publication Data
Roth, Susan L.
Hands around the library : protecting Egypt's treasured books /
by Susan L. Roth and Karen Leggett Abouraya ; collages by Susan L. Roth.
p.   cm.
ISBN 978-0-8037-3747-1 (hardcover)
1. Aliksandrina (Library)—History—Juvenile literature. 2. Libraries—Egypt—Alexandria—Juvenile literature.
3. Libraries—Destruction and pillage—Egypt—Alexandria—Juvenile literature.
4. Cultural property—Protection—Juvenile literature. 5. Egypt—History—21st century—Juvenile literature.
I. Abouraya, Karen Leggett. II. Title.
Z858.A48R68 2012   962.053—dc23   2011038198

About the graphic leit motifs:

The photo-montage backgrounds on the book flaps, the end papers, and on the last spread of the story proper were inspired by the huge 500-alphabet graphic of the granite wall on the face of the library.

The bright-colored, appliquéd quilt motifs, used as decoration in the front and back matter and in the librarian's head covering, were inspired by the tents often found on the streets in present-day Egypt, for use in celebrations such as weddings.

The ever-changing juxtaposition of the protestors' signs defined my vision of the marchers and I therefore chose it as the overriding graphic element for most of the collages in this book.

Thank you to:

Tharwat Abouraya, for his Arabic translations and for sharing his cultural sensibilities; Adam Abouraya, for his excellent photographs; Nadia Abouraya, for her invaluable help preparing the photographs; Shaimaa Saad, for the generous sharing of her unique primary source information about the Bibliotheca Alexandrina and the actual protests in Alexandria, in which she participated.

Appalachian State University (Margaret Gregor, Kate Johnson, Jeanne Lawrence, Jenny McCourry, Gary and Kathy Moorman, Mary Reichel); Burgundy Farm Country Day School (Ann Van Deusen and her students), Alexandria, Virginia; Dial Books for Young Readers (Kate Harrison, Lauri Hornik, Lily Malcom, Jasmin Rubero); Forest Knolls Elementary School, Silver Spring, Maryland (Susan Osmun, David Airozo, and their students); Olga Guartan; Betsy Kraft; Nancy Patz; Alana Roth; Jesse Roth; Kholoud Said; Anna Struk; Rym Ibrahim; Cindy Woodruff.